Girl In The Mirror

Mirror

A Teen's Guide To Self Awareness

By
Denise Crittendon

Girl In The Mirror

Copyright © 2000 Denise Crittendon

ISBN 1-888754-06-0
Library of Congress Catalog Card Number: 00-135580

Produced & Published
For
Denise Crittendon

By
Detroit Writer's Guild, Inc.
PO Box 23100
Detroit, MI 48223

Peggy A. Moore — *Founder*
Heather Buchanan — *Chairperson, Board of Directors*
Herbert R. Metoyer — *Executive Director/Editor & Typesetter*

To Order:
Call 248-352-0990
or visit
www.GirlInTheMirror.com

Cover Photograph by Gordon Alexander
Abstract Design by Moses Harris
Cover Design by Herbert R. Metoyer

The Detroit Writer's Guild is a non-profit literary organization. Its primary goals are to improve literary awareness, train & encourage aspiring authors, showcase samples of their work, preserve African-American Heritage, and increase participation in the Cultural Arts.

Printed in the United States of America

*To my nieces, Rhonda and Shannon
and to the girls at Vista Maria Girls' Home.*

*May you always have the courage
to pursue your dreams.*

— Acknowledgements —

A special thanks to Chuck Smith for helping to make this publication possible. Thanks also to Carl Collins of Charity Motors, Inc. and African American Parent Magazine for helping to sponsor the project. In addition, I would like to thank Dave Steele and Nick VanZanten of Lutheran Social Services of Michigan; Kathy Adams of Katherine Enterprises, Inc.; Herb Metoyer of the Detroit Writer's Guild; artist Moses Harris; proofreader Sharon McIntire; photographer, Gordon Alexander; Alyssa Martina and Alexis Bourkoulas of Metro Parent Publishing Group, John Creighton and cover models (left to right) Johnell Jones, Carrie Thompson, Linh Dang and Emily Happy Miller. I also would like to extend a special "Thank you," to Pattie Yerke who helped launch my own journey to self awareness, my mother Nellie Crittendon, my father, Roy Crittendon, and every person who believed in and supported this endeavor.

CONTENTS

———

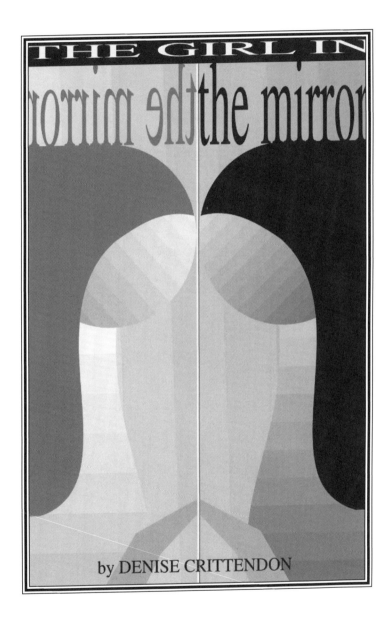
THE GIRL IN the mirror

by DENISE CRITTENDON

"But he, taking her by the hand cried out saying
Girl Arise!"
Luke 8:54

Introduction —

~ ~ ~

Have you ever tossed a shiny penny into a pond and made a secret wish?

What kind of wish did you make? Did you wish you were rich or did you wish for super stardom? Did you wish for better grades, more friends and an appearance and personality so fantastic that everyone stopped and took notice?

If you did, you are not alone. Wishes are kind of contagious. Most people, young and old, enjoy the good feeling that goes along with wishing and hoping and fantasizing.

Many people, however, don't know how to make those wishes a reality. This might come as a surprise to many, but it really is possible for anyone — even a teen-age girl — to change her world completely.

The good life is not make believe. Everyone — including you — has the capacity to turn stumbling blocks into stepping stones. You can have a life filled with happiness and a spirit filled with love and peace. You can do anything you want to do and be anything you want to be.

All you have to do is get out of the chicken coop.

It could be that you are one of a number of teens who are dreaming, exploring possibilities, searching for answers and looking for more out of life. You want to know how to grow further; how to fulfill all of your desires and build a future of wealth, spirituality and harmony.

Or you could be stuck in a rut, strutting about in a place or predicament where you don't belong. Could be you were born there or it could be you ended up in your unfavorable situation quite by accident. But that doesn't mean you are trapped.

My favorite folk story is about an egg that rolls out of an eagle's nest perched high on a hilltop. That egg tumbles more than one hundred feet to the ground below and, somehow, manages to land in the middle of a barnyard filled with a bunch of clucking chickens.

Eventually, it cracks open and out bounces a baby eagle. Of

1

course, the chickens don't know what this strange bird is and they don't care. It grows along with the rest of the hatchlings and does its best to mingle and become one of the crowd.

That is not an easy job. For one thing, this peculiar newcomer doesn't look like the scruffy little chicks. However, it follows the direction of its peers and scampers around the farm, pecking and scratching the dirt. But, inside, it senses something isn't right. It feels out of it sometimes. At other times, it gets this weird feeling that it doesn't quite fit in. Every now and then, it pauses, gazes up at the sky and marvels at the eagles soaring high over the barn. It is in awe of these majestic creatures and wishes it could spread its wings and fly.

But it never flies because it never realizes that it is an eagle.

Could it be that you too are an eagle? Take a moment now and ask yourself these questions: What is your true identity? Are you really being you or is there a better you, a more positive, happier you fighting to be born?

The answer is yes. And now is the time for you to claim your birthright. Know that you already are the stuff you dream about. Understand that you really are all that and more.

From time to time, say to yourself "Girl, you've got it going on." Gaze into the mirror. The girl staring back at you represents your memories, your spirit, your good and bad characteristics. Deep down, you understand that it isn't totally up to your family, your parents or your guidance counselor to change your life. It is up to you — The Girl in the Mirror. It is up to you to look yourself in the eyes and declare that you are ready to take control of your own destiny.

Then pat yourself on the back and thank yourself for all the things you are doing right. Don't wait for other people to do it. A compliment is a compliment — whether it comes from you or from someone else.

You are your own hidden treasure. You have a mighty power dwelling within you; the power and love and strength of God. This power is a guiding force. If you nurture it by believing in yourself and refusing to give up, guess what will happen?

Soon, you will be flying like an eagle. Pretty soon, you will find yourself achieving your highest goals and living the kind of life that will make your parents proud. What's more important, you will be proud and that's the best feeling of all.

You see, it's like this: Things go wrong sometimes. It could be something that occurs early in your life or it could be something that happens later. It doesn't matter when the problems appear. It does matter what you do about them.

If you spend your life pouting or acting out because you didn't receive something you expected, you are like the six-year-old who wastes her entire day at the carnival, crying and whining because she didn't get a candy apple when she first arrived. Are you willing to miss out on the joy of life just because you didn't get what you wanted right away?

I certainly hope not. In this book, you are going to learn how to wipe away the crocodile tears of a child and start facing the world like a strong, happy teen who knows how to work it.

You are going to be given the spiritual tools of love, prayer, forgiveness, gratitude and affirmation. You will be shown how to use those tools to carve a new reality for yourself.

You will learn to recognize just how outstanding you really are. The exercises in this book will convince you that anything anyone else can do, YOU CAN do. There is no such thing as can't; so throw that word out of your vocabulary. With a double dose of determination and self confidence, you will find that YOU CAN earn good grades, YOU CAN develop close relationships, YOU CAN deal with the ups and downs of everyday living and YOU CAN learn to look for positive rather than negative role models. YOU CAN attract good times, wonderful companions, money and success!

You are entitled to it! You are the guest of honor at a major feast. It is called life. Welcome. Now, step up to the table and help yourself. Mind your manners and, please, be careful what you wish for.

Odds are, it's going to come true.

In Love and Peace,

Denise Crittendon

Chapter One

You Thought Yourself Into It
You Can Think Yourself Out Of It

"When I go out on the ice, there are good thoughts and there are bad thoughts . . . The bad thoughts are there. You just have to push them away." (Tara Lipinski, Gold Medallist/Figure skater)

———

How would you react if I handed you a scorching hot potato? Let's say this is a sizzling potato, straight from the oven. Let's pretend right now that I am placing it in your bare hands. What would you do?

You would drop it. You would probably yell something like: "Ooouuch! It's hot!" Then you'd let it go so fast more than likely it would splatter all over the floor.

That's where the expression "she dropped him like a hot potato" originates. Everyone knows that you can't hold a hot potato in your hand for long.

But everyone doesn't seem to know that you cannot and should not hold on to those hot, burning negative thoughts.

Negative thoughts are defeating thoughts like "I'll never be able to do this," or "That boy isn't interested in me so I must not be good enough," or "I don't like the way my body looks." Negative thoughts are bad memories that we play over and over in our minds. Negative thoughts are hot potatoes. They sting and when that happens we need to handle them just like we would if they

5

touched the palms of our hands. We let them go.

In her hit song, "Let It Flow," Toni Braxton reminds us that love is supposed to feel good and that when it doesn't we're being unfair to ourselves if we don't just "Let it go," and "Let it flow." The same attitude applies to most situations in life. It is called taking control of your own mind. And that, my friends, is what you have the power to do.

God has given each and every one of us the power of a free will. That means that the thoughts in a positive mind are there by choice. Everyone sometimes battles with negative, uncomfortable emotions. However, a girl who believes in herself does not allow them to dominate her. She may feel bad awhile. Before long, she is shrugging and sighing "Whatever!" She releases the woe-is-me thoughts because they don't feel good and she wants to feel good. She likes herself and she wants to treat herself well. She knows that she is not being good to herself when she allows her mind to be filled with burdensome, painful feelings.

They are hot potatoes which we kick out of our minds before they scorch our spirit. We get rid of them as quickly as possible because they hurt. We also do it because we realize that negative thoughts attract negative experiences. The more we think about sad things, the more sad things happen. The more we say negative things about ourselves to ourselves, the worse we feel about ourselves.

Instead of hot potatoes, we need to pump ourselves up by thinking about the things that put us in a good mood. We need to spend a lot of time reminding ourselves of the good times. We need to tell ourselves something good is about to happen again. And if something bad is happening, we need to first remind ourselves of the tremendous power of our spirit and then tell ourselves that we are children of God, capable of surviving and overcoming any crisis.

You can handle whatever is happening simply by changing your thoughts about it. All you have to do is pay attention to what you are thinking then change those thoughts. It might seem difficult at first. But force yourself. When you have a sad thought, immediately think about something pleasant. Remember a volleyball game, a fun time with a boyfriend, the time you were recognized for something you achieved in school. Then think about it, think about it, think about it. Get behind the wheel of your mind and steer.

But the problem is that some of us have been holding on to the hot potatoes for so long, they feel natural to us. We're used to the discomfort of not believing in the best. We may not want bad habits, but we've grown accustomed to them and they feel as cozy as an old shoe. How can we overcome these feelings?

We can say affirmations. An affirmation is a positive statement about yourself and your life. It is a powerful statement in the present tense about something you want in your life now. It is something you say with feeling and meaning. You declare it as if it is the total truth. For example:

I AM BEAUTIFUL INSIDE AND OUT AND I DESERVE THE BEST LIFE HAS TO OFFER

I AM GIFTED AND I AM TALENTED

I AM PRECIOUS AND I AM LOVED

When repeated, affirmations have a powerful effect on us and they can change our lives. A girl who is down and out would gradually begin to feel inspired if she were to tell herself over and over that she is a precious and worthy human being. Affirmations chase out old thoughts. They make you smile. They perk you up in the morning. I've counseled teens who have said that affirmations help them get through the day.

The best way to understand it is to think about the effect they have on the brain. Keep in mind that the brain is like a muscle. You might do crunches to strengthen stomach muscles or bicep curls to strengthen muscles in your arms. In much the same way, affirmations strengthen the brain. When you exercise the arms or legs, you rely on repetition. The repeated motion builds the muscle.

When you exercise the mind, you also rely on repetition. Affirmations, which are positive statements said over and over again everyday, build strong healthy minds. They make you confident and they rid your mind of those unhealthy, hot potato thoughts. What's more, they can become a permanent way of thinking. After several months of positive affirmations, you will begin to believe anything you are programming yourself to believe.

The brain is made of a network of little pathways that look sort of like wiggly tunnels. Each new affirmation creates a strong new path in your mind. If you'd like, you can think of your brain as a computer and your affirmations as the new program you are choosing to install.

Constantly tell yourself that no one is in charge of your thoughts but you. That means no one has the power to tell you what to think or feel — but you. So be careful. What you think about with feeling really does happen. Just wait awhile and, I promise, you really can and will have whatever you are focusing on. You will become a magnet for whatever you want. What will it be? Clear, beautiful skin? New clothes? Good grades? Lots of friends? The opportunity to go to college? A wonderful career one day as a doctor, an accountant, a police officer, a dental hygienist, a lawyer, a hair stylist or a nurse?

Hold those thoughts and believe in them like you know with certainty that they are going to happen. And they will. Now, this does not apply to requests to change the behavior and/or attitude of another person. Everyone has his or her own road in life and that cannot be changed by you.

In other words, you can't make your brother or sister do something the way you want them to do it just because you're thinking it. Also, if you like a certain boy at school, thinking about him won't guarantee a love connection between the two of you. Why? Because that might be violating his destiny or interfering with his wishes. (For all you know, he could be praying to be with Mariah Carey.)

What you have to do is pray with a believing heart for a special friend, then make a list of the qualities you would like your friend to possess. The boy you like can pray to meet Mariah Carey but, unless he is dating her, he can't expect to marry her.

When it comes to relationships, don't be that specific! You can't ask for Joe Shmoe, John Smith or even Humpty Dumpty. But you can ask to meet a dream person with certain characteristics and you will meet him.

So, are you ready for a better life? Do you really want to think yourself out of the conditions you are in at this moment? Do you want to become electrically charged with happy thoughts and magnetized for good things?

On the next page, you'll find a list of positive affirmations. They are the vitamins you will depend on to boost your mental workout.

9

Don't worry. It won't hurt and you won't be sore in the morning. You are simply getting your thoughts into shape.

All you have to do is relax, take a deep breath and follow a few easy instructions.

Are you ready? One, two and three. Let's begin!

———

AFFIRMATIONS EXERCISE

1. There are all kinds of ways to use affirmations. They are spiritual tools that can lead you to a wonderful, new life. Pick the ones that best fit your situation. Try writing them in large letters on index cards and placing them on your dresser (so you can read them daily). You might want to say them over and over every morning in the shower or say them silently to yourself throughout the day. Say each one three times, before moving on to the next one. Remember, repetition builds muscle. So if you want to get mentally fit, say your affirmations everyday.

I AM A MAGNET FOR POSITIVE, HAPPY SITUATIONS.

I AM ENJOYING A FABULOUS LIFE.

I LOVE MY LIFE JUST THE WAY IT IS AND IT IS GETTING BETTER AND BETTER ALL THE TIME.

GOD APPROVES OF ME AND I APPROVE OF MYSELF.

I LOVE MY BODY JUST THE WAY IT IS AND IT IS GETTING BETTER ALL THE TIME.

I AM WORTHY FOR I AM A PRECIOUS CHILD OF GOD.

THE WORLD IS MY CANVAS. I AM CREATING ALL THAT I WANT AND I AM MAKING ALL OF MY WISHES COME TRUE.

I Am A Very Good Student With Goals And Purpose.

I Am Precious And I Am Loved.

I Am Gifted And I Am Talented.

I Am Beautiful Inside And Out And I Deserve The Best Life Has To Offer.

I Am Beautiful Inside And Out And I Deserve To Be Treated With Love And Respect.

I Release My Past. I Am Healed And My Heart Is Filled With Self Love.

I Deserve The Best And I Expect The Best.

I Am Holding My Head Up For I Am On My Way Up.

I Forgive My Past. I Cherish Myself And I See Only Good.

I Honor God's Temple. I Keep My Thoughts Loving, Positive And Peaceful.

I Am Happy, I Am Healthy And I Am Positive.

I Am Happy And My Life Is The Bomb!

I Can Feel God's Loving Presence And I Feel Peace.

I Am A Success And I Am Living My Dreams.

I Truly Love And Value Myself.

I Am Attractive. I Am Unique. I Am Important.

I Have Let Go And I Am Letting God Bless Me.

———

2. What do you want to claim? Write five of your own affirmations. Avoid using negative words. Make sure your affirmations are positive and in the present tense.

K - I have people, family friends that want the best for me.

K - I am Smart

K - I am prode of the People I come from

★ K - I have talents be·ond my wildest Dreams ★

K - I have my own cheerleads and I woud no change my life for anything

13

Chapter Two

SELF LOVE IS YOUR CREDIT CARD

"The easiest way to live with yourself in this big, scary world is to love yourself. I know it sounds corny but you got to love yourself." (Julia Roberts, actress)

———

Have you ever wondered why Brandy's eyes sparkle or why Vanessa Williams always seems to be flashing a bright, beautiful smile?

They are thinking the right thoughts. They are focusing on joyful feelings, and positive emotions. They know what they want out of life and they know how to make it happen.

It's obvious that both Brandy and Vanessa are confident about their bodies and about their abilities. Watch the way they walk and the self-assured manner in which they carry themselves. They know they've got it going on and they understand that a good attitude is the best makeup.

They realize that they are only as beautiful as their own thoughts.

Brandy and Vanessa appear to know instinctively that our faces broadcast what we are thinking. They know that worry thoughts etch worry lines on the face and thoughts that reek of jealousy leave even deeper indentations. On the other hand, thoughts of happiness and enthusiasm are uplifting. They massage our spirit on the inside and brighten our faces on the outside.

Think about it. When you're sad, you're frowning. When you're upset, you're scowling. It's almost as if you made a Freddie Krueger mask and glued it right on top of your face.

Most of us don't realize that our thoughts have such an enormous power over the way we look. We're almost as bad as ostriches. Unlike the ostrich, we know that everyone can see us, no matter where our heads are hidden. But in some ways human behavior is similar. We believe that just because no one can see those quiet rumblings in our mind that, perhaps, we can bury them. However, we cannot.

The ideas in our minds help make us who we are. Outer beauty is often a magnificent symbol of what is going on deep in the soul. This doesn't always mean that if God blessed you with a naturally beautiful face, that automatically you have a beautiful spirit and it doesn't necessarily mean that if a girl seems unattractive then she must be ugly inside. It means that the girl who may appear unattractive at first will have an awesome glow if her thoughts are in the right place. People will look at her with approval and say "there is something about her." Vice versa for the attractive girl. She can smear on all the lipstick and nail polish she wants but if her attitude is messed up, people will see through her sooner or later.

People will walk right past her to talk to the girl who understands that her true beauty lies in what she is thinking about 24 hours a day.

What does a beautiful girl think about? She thinks kind thoughts about others and she lavishes kind thoughts upon herself. That's right! She praises others and she praises herself. She says nice things to herself about herself.

The beautiful girl is the one who is filled with self respect and self love.

When you love yourself, you are generally happy because you like the way you feel inside. It feels good to be loved doesn't it? When others love us, we eagerly accept their love and we enjoy it.

The love we feel for ourselves is just as comforting. Loving ourselves allows us to tap into the divine love that God is feeling for us. Loving ourselves is a way of appreciating our own uniqueness. It is a way of acknowledging that we were specially created by God for a special purpose on Earth. It is our way of saying God gave us life for a reason. Therefore, God gave each and every one of us a certain amount of abilities and talents.

In fact, God has given us everything we need to pursue our personal goals during our lifetimes. Did you know that no two snowflakes are exactly alike? Each one is very distinct and so are humans. We are all blessed with different strengths and talents. Yet it is up to us to determine what makes us individual and how we can best use those special qualities.

It's not a bad idea to make a list of what you approve of about yourself and what doesn't meet your approval. Give yourself credit for the qualities you do like. Tell yourself that they are gifts from God and ask yourself how you are going to enhance those gifts.

As far as the qualities you don't like, well that's easy. First of all, accept them. They are part of you and no one is perfect. The more you acknowledge that fact, the easier it will be to admit that you could stand some improvement. Believe that you can change and you will. But first, tell yourself "I love myself just the way I am and I am getting better all the time."

As a child of God, it is important that we send ourselves those loving thoughts every day. This might seem weird at first, but it's not a bad idea to look in the mirror everyday and tell yourself "I Love You." It's a way of honoring yourself. It's a way of loving God's presence within you and giving ongoing thanks to God. It's also a way of letting God shine through you.

The more we become aware of our own glory, the more our eyes will sparkle like Brandy and the more our smiles will radiate like Vanessa Williams.

The opposite happens when girls don't care enough about themselves. They walk around in a funk all the time and sometimes they put themselves down. Some will even overcompensate by pretending they think they are "all that." They brag. They engage in self destructive behavior. They do anything to get attention.

But it's all smoke and hot air. In some cases, these girls will go to the extreme and waste a good deal of energy making negative comments about other people. And it's all because, they don't really like themselves. They may put up a good front. However, on the inside, they are saying negative things to themselves about themselves. They really don't like who they are and they try to make themselves feel better by looking down on their peers.

Do you know someone who behaves like that? Are you like that at times? If you are, don't feel embarrassed and whatever you do don't beat up on yourself. Just keep repeating: "I love myself just the way I am and I am getting better and better all the time."

The girl who loves herself accepts herself. She understands that everyone will not like her and that is okay. Some people like stir-fried broccoli and others prefer corn on the cob. That certainly doesn't imply that a stalk of broccoli should become jealous of an ear of corn. Each vegetable has an individual taste and appearance. Each provides different nutrients for the body. And each will have its share of fans who swear they eat it everyday and enemies who refuse to go near the stuff.

Do you get the point? It could be that you have the sweetness and sleekness of corn. So don't worry if someone you were trying to befriend is ignoring you or if the boy you like in your math class isn't interested. Maybe they don't like corn. But many people do. Many people can and will appreciate you for who you are.

Yet, that appreciation absolutely must begin within you. Others can react to you any way they choose. But, you and only you are the one with the power to make your eyes light up. And you are the only one who can produce a smile that will make your entire face glow.

How? Notice the next time you meet someone with genuine self respect and figure it out. Make her your own personal role model. Study her. How does she carry herself? What kinds of things does she say?

She probably gives other people compliments. That's because her mind is filled with compliments. She is generous with her compliments to others because she is generous with her compliments to herself. She is kind and considerate to others because she is kind and considerate to herself. She loves others because she loves herself.

She has a friendly personality because she is happy and turned on by all of her positive thoughts. True self love is the result of loving your own thoughts. If your thoughts are angry and filled with jealousy or self doubt, you're not going to love them very much are you? Definitely not! In fact, you would be in so much turmoil, you probably wouldn't enjoy your own company. Why? You wouldn't want to be alone with your own thoughts. Often, when you don't like what you are thinking about, you don't like yourself. When you like your thoughts, you are excited about who you are.

You will pat yourself on the back and maybe give yourself a high five. You will smile a lot. You will never forget to look into your own eyes, hug yourself and say "I Love You!"

Believe it or not, whispering "I Love You" to yourself is one of the most powerful acts a teenager, or anyone of any age, can perform. Number one, if you don't love yourself, you really aren't going to believe anyone else can love you. Number two, when you love yourself you develop a loving, positive attitude about others.

What if you were working as a salesgirl in a store that had a rack of Guess jeans and another rack stuffed with off-brand jeans that were poorly designed? If a customer walked in with a couple of hundred dollars, do you think you would have any problem convincing that customer which jeans to buy?

I seriously doubt it. If you're selling designer clothes, you don't have to badmouth the rest of the merchandise. The popular brand speaks for itself. The same thing applies to people who have a healthy self-esteem. If they honestly feel good about who they are, they have no need to judge, criticize or put down anyone else.

Remember that the next time you get the urge to knock someone else. You are not being loving to yourself when you make nasty remarks about others.

When you free yourself from the hang-up of belittling your peers, you are taking your first step down the road of self-worth. Finally, you are beginning to love yourself for who you really are. As a consequence, you are loving others — just as they are.

Nothing is more powerful than a loving thought. If you keep your mind filled with wonderful messages about yourself, you won't waste time thinking or saying bad things about anyone.

Your attitude will change. You will blossom and become more confident. And many of the blessings you have been praying for will begin to happen. That's because Self Love is like a credit card. It is your ticket to anything you want in life.

So go ahead, tell yourself "I look good today!" Look up at the sky and notice what a gorgeous day it really is. Mention to yourself that you're a fun person to hang out with. Remind yourself of how pretty you look when your hair is styled just the way you like it.

Try it! Everyday, say something kind to that person called "Me, Myself and I." Treat yourself as if you deserve the very best out of life.

After all, if you don't believe in you, who will?

———

LOVE EXERCISE

1. Make a list of your positive, personal qualities and traits, the ones you really feel good about. Include both physical and spiritual attributes.

2. Make a list of the people you don't like or people you don't think are very pleasant to be around. After each name, write down something positive about that person. Everyone has the spirit of God within them. Everyone has worthwhile qualities. What nice comments can you make about the individuals on your list?

3. Think of someone you have criticized in the past. Block out any feelings of criticism and replace them with a kind remark about yourself. For instance, write: "Instead of criticizing *you know who*, I would rather focus on my…(Insert your special qualities and other gifts from God.)"

Chapter Three

PROBLEMS ARE OPPORTUNITIES
TURNED UPSIDE DOWN

"God doesn't put you through things. He pulls you through them." (Kirk Franklin, gospel singer)

———

When L.L. Cool J. was a kid he suffered so much abuse in his home that he became determined he would never have to live in pain again. He turned his life around because he focused, worked hard and had faith in a power greater than himself.

Actress Jada Pinkett-Smith had to deal with similar challenges as a child. Her home life wasn't cool and she started running around with a bad crowd. Then Jada changed and developed an unbeatable attitude. She was good friends with late rapper Tupac Shakur and the two decided that bad times could be a sign of a powerful destiny.

Jada held on to that belief and used her streetwise spunk and sassy confidence to lead her down the road to success. She traded her acting out on the streets for acting on the screen. She transformed her hard life into a wonderful life and a glamorous career as an actress.

Ditto for Tupac. He was able to live out the exciting adventures he rapped about. However he eventually was murdered while

25

living the life he believed in. Unlike Jada, Tupac never let go of the grit and drama of his stormy past. He never broke free from his painful cocoon and, consequently, he never reached for something more peaceful and positive.

That something is a Faith that God can and will make a difference in our lives. Kirk Franklin and the singer, Jewel, are also examples of successful people who allowed spiritual guidance to lead them to their dreams.

They are modern day symbols of the power of Faith and they are constant reminders that God doesn't permit problems to occur in our lives because He wants us to suffer. God allows problems in the hopes that we will see them for what they are:

Opportunities turned upside down.

Problems are God's way of saying "Yo, wake up and do something different!" If you have a problem, you better believe God is trying to get your attention.

Mirta de Perales, a self-made millionaire in Miami, says that when she was growing up in Cuba she faced more problems than she can remember. For starters, her playmates teased her because she contracted an illness that caused her hair to fall out. Because of her dilemma, she became interested in gaining as much knowledge as she could about hair.

Later, her father died and her mother moved out of town to find work. Mirta figured God had inspired her to learn about hair care because that skill would help her to support the family. Instead of feeling bad about her mom being gone, she looked for and found a blessing.

The town her mother lived in was miles away and she could only afford to send $20 a month home to the family. Mirta, who was 12 years old, was able to earn three times that amount by styling hair for the wealthy women in her community. She turned

26

her problem into a miraculous blessing.

By the time she was a young adult, she was a rich woman. Years later, political and social unrest erupted in Cuba and Mirta was forced to flee the country, leaving everything she had worked for behind.

She arrived in the United States with only five dollars in her pocket. But she maintained a sunny disposition and a heart filled with hope. Eventually, she opened hair salons and developed a hair care line that amassed a fortune. She now runs a million-dollar beauty empire and enjoys telling stories about the "miracles" in her life.

Mirta is proof that God works in mysterious ways. Her experience serves as evidence that just because everything isn't going just the way you want it, doesn't mean God isn't on your side.

For example, you might be upset that you are on punishment. Or you might be disappointed because you weren't allowed to go to a party, the movies or some other outing with your friends.

A "No" can be a blessing. Just like a mother won't allow her two-year-old to touch a hot iron, God won't allow us to do certain things when they are not for our higher good.

We are God's children and, often, we just can't understand why something has happened. But, sometimes things go wrong in order for things to go right. Martial artist Bruce Lee once said that we must "Adapt to whatever situation is before us." We must become spiritual warriors — tough enough in our faith in God that we know how to make every circumstance work to our advantage.

Let's say it's a nice day and you have been given strict orders to remain in the house. Maybe it's unfair. Maybe it isn't. But it's up to you to make the best of it.

You could use that time to make a phone call to someone you haven't had the opportunity to talk to in awhile. You could spend time with a little brother or sister. Or you could catch up on some homework and get ahead in at least one of your classes in school. You may not like the situation but if you look hard enough you almost always will find something good.

What if, for instance, you get a zit in the middle of your face right at the time that you are planning for a very special evening? What could possibly be right about something so wrong? Or even worse, what if you are betrayed by a boyfriend or close friend you really trusted? How could either of these experiences lead to anything positive?

Sad circumstances (especially the real painful ones like illness or a death in the family) aren't always easy to explain. No one but God knows why certain situations occur in our lives. Major tragedies are God's will and usually aren't easy to deal with or to figure out.

But even they sometimes can have the power to affect our lives in truly miraculous ways. (Some people go back to school, start new careers, get off drugs or discover new talents after something awful has really startled them and shaken up their lives.) Experiences on a smaller scale have a different impact. Possibly, minor upsets like zits are meant to teach us how to stop being so sensitive about what people say and think. Perhaps, God is teaching us how to toughen up now so that we will be able to cope with something else that may happen later down the road. Or, believe it or not, it actually might be meant for us to stay home that night.

The reasons things happen are too numerous to list on one page; but you get the idea. Some so-called problems that may seem terrible one day, don't always seem like such a big deal when we look back at them months later. In fact, sometimes we look back at something and we're actually glad it happened. (We might be glad we broke up with one person because if we hadn't we never would have met someone else we liked so much better.)

And here's the amazing news: Getting in trouble can have the same effect. Suppose you get sent to detention at school or you get accused of doing something wrong at home. The punishment and other consequences of your actions may encourage you to work on improving your attitude.

You might meet a cool counselor who takes an interest in you and gives you renewed hope. Or you might feel so bad about your actions that you make a vow never to repeat that behavior again.

The same thing can happen when someone criticizes you unfairly. Instead of getting depressed and agreeing with your critic, do something you have always wanted to do but never got around to it. Try out for the cheer team, write a poem or join a choir and prove how really talented you are.

The artist Prince said he was distraught when he faced difficulties with a company that once handled his music. Later, when he ended his recording contract with that particular company, he moved on to a different one. Under the new label, his creativity flourished so much that he felt like writing his former company a thank you letter.

In other words, if something is bothering you today, you might be laughing about it next week. If something is bothering you next week, it might be your stepping stone to better days ahead. If something is bothering you during the days ahead, that something might be the very thing that gives you the strength to improve your life. But first, you must have strong Faith.

How do you develop Faith? By refusing to believe in those situations called problems and making up your mind that, like Mirta, like Jewel, and like L.L. Cool J., you too can be a miracle worker.

You must believe that if things are going wrong, opportunity must be knocking. With that attitude, you'll always be enthusiastic and optimistic, no matter what is going on.

———

OPPORTUNITY EXERCISE

1. Make a list of the situations in your life that you consider problems. Next to each situation, write down something positive that could develop as a result of that experience. Be optimistic!

2. How many things went wrong this week? How did you handle it. Write a little note, detailing what happened and how you reacted. Now that you are looking back on that situation, can you find something good to say about it? Write down anything joyful that could result from this week's problems.

3. Have you ever had an experience you didn't like that turned out to be a blessing in disguise? Write about it. Explain what you learned.

(Whenever you are feeling doubtful, remember this experience and say to yourself: "I trust God. It might seem as if life is serving me lemons but I don't know what God is stirring up in my life. God might be making lemonade.")

*C*hapter *Four*

KEEPING THE FAITH

"I don't believe it's possible that I won't succeed." (Venus Williams, tennis champion)

———

Are you feeling excited right now? Are you looking forward to anything in particular?

What if I told you that tomorrow your favorite aunt was going to visit you and surprise you with a $500 bill? I know what you're thinking right now. Yeah right! But I want you to pretend. Just pretend for a moment that what I am saying is true. You do have a rich aunt and she is planning to present you with the gift of $500.

Now, let's go back to our original questions: Are you feeling excited right now? Are you looking forward to anything in particular?

I'll bet your answers have changed dramatically. Suddenly you can say "Sure, I'm excited. Hey, I can't wait until tomorrow. I know I got it going on!"

Now, here's yet another question: Why can't you get excited like that all the time? Let's say you don't know anyone who is rich or let's say you do but you know he or she isn't preparing to give you a large sum of money. It shouldn't matter. You can and should walk around in a state of joy anyway.

Whatever you do, don't walk around thinking you don't have

anything to feel good about. If you are entertaining those kinds of thoughts, you are setting your standards low. Consequently, you are probably waking up every morning expecting nothing special from your day.

But you have to ask yourself which state of mind feels best. Didn't it feel good just to think that $500 was on the way? Did you feel charged and happy and hopeful? That is what I call tapping into the power of Faith.

For some of us that is difficult to do. We're afraid that if we have faith in something and it doesn't happen, we're going to feel let down and disappointed. So we don't bother believing. That way, we figure, we are protecting ourselves.

Instead, look at it this way: If you do get the results you hoped for, you'll feel great. If it doesn't happen, at least you felt good waiting for it to happen.

Okay, so now you're probably thinking, "Has the author of this book lost it or what?" You're probably saying "Get real!" That's a good suggestion. We should all get real, meaning we should all get real connected to the real power of real faith.

Real faith is that ability to let go of your worries and turn them all over to God.

I once heard an interesting story about a girl who went shopping and fell in love with a dress she couldn't afford. The next day she told her girlfriend: "I just tried on this sharp dress but I didn't have the money for it." Her friend told her that God answered all prayers and that God would somehow help her get that dress if she wanted it. She advised her to pray and pray and pray.

And so she did. Every morning, she clasped her hands together, gazed heavenward and said "Please God, I really need that dress."

Every night, she got down on her knees and said the same prayer. At the end of the month, she went back to her friend. She didn't have the dress, but she did have an attitude.

"I can't believe I even wasted my time like that," she complained. "I knew I wasn't going to get that dress."

Of course, she didn't get the dress. Her prayers weren't answered simply because she never believed in them in the first place. When you pray about a matter you must make sure you have a believing heart.

That's the purpose of the affirmations we began practicing in the first chapter. We use affirmations to give our prayers that extra cushion of support. Affirmations give our prayers backbone. When we say affirmations, we are in the process of convincing ourselves that this request can become a reality. As a result, we become more passionate and hopeful about whatever it is we are trying to change in our lives.

Remember, life is one gigantic smorgasbord and you are a privileged guest of honor. The reason we don't always have what we want is that we fret too much. We give our problems to God then we worry so much we never really allow God to handle it.

Suppose you bought a brand new skirt. You like this skirt a lot but it is far too long to wear. You might not like to sew but you have a good friend whose mom taught her how to hem all sorts of clothing. She's so good at it that you give her the skirt and tell her you need it back in a week.

She promises to have it ready. But the next day, you call her and ask how she's coming. She laughs and says she has plenty of time. You say okay but you call back the next day and the next. Then you find out she hasn't even started hemming the skirt so you stop by her house and ask to have it back.

You try to put the hem in yourself but you botch it up and

end up taking the skirt back to your girlfriend. She's a good sport and agrees to finish the hem. But you start the same behavior all over again. You call. You complain. You bug her constantly and before long you return to her house and announce that you've changed your mind. You believe you can do the job yourself.

The next day, your friend can't believe her eyes. There you stand, in tears, asking her if she'll hem your skirt. By the time the week is up, you are one frustrated girl. The hem still isn't in the skirt. You're sad and frazzled and hurt. Your girlfriend didn't finish and you feel like she didn't keep her promise.

The truth is you never let her keep her promise. You kept worrying, constantly bugging her and interfering with the process. How could she fix the skirt when you continually took it back?

That is exactly what we do when we give God our concerns. We pray and ask God to fix the confusion in our lives. Then we keep harping on and on about it. We fret. We complain. We take it back.

God can't help us because we never let go. Having faith means we're ready to take that dare. We're ready to truly let go and let God hem our problems.

If you're still having a hard time with this, go outside one night and look at the stars and the moon. Notice how bright and awesome they are and then ask yourself who holds them there in place night after night after night.

Once you answer this question I guarantee you'll relax a bit. Hopefully, you'll climb into bed and remember a bit of advice you've probably heard all of your life:

Keep The Faith!

———

FAITH EXERCISE

1. Go outside and look up at the sky. There is no ceiling. Allow this simple act to serve as a reminder that the possibilities in your life are endless. There is no ceiling for what you can become. The only limitations are the ones you accept or create yourself.

2. Have you ever worried and felt sure that something was going to go wrong only to have things actually work out very well? Have you ever been extremely worried about a circumstance or person, or afraid that a situation would turn into a disaster? Try to remember these incidents. Do you feel as if you worried for nothing? Write a brief sentence or two describing your fears. Next write a few sentences explaining how well everything turned out.

3. Have you ever felt like giving up on something, then suddenly decided to try one last time? Are you glad you did? Did you succeed because you refused to give up? What did you learn from this experience?

Chapter Five

CRUISIN' YOUR IMAGINATION

"I visualized where I wanted to be, what kind of player I wanted to become." *(Michael Jordan, NBA Star)*

———

Stop what you are doing at this moment and make believe you are somewhere else doing something you enjoy. Close your eyes and picture yourself strolling along a beach, performing with the cheerleading squad or on the dance floor, kicking it with your best friends.

If you're at the lake or ocean, imagine you can feel the warm moisture in the air and hear the waves rushing against the shore.

If you're working out with the cheer team, see the scoreboard light up, get into the excitement, hear the crowd roaring in the background as a throng of ballplayers race across the gym.

If you're pretending to be at a party, you might feel the vibrations of loud music. Notice all the kids around you, clowning around, smiling, laughing and having a good time.

Now, open your eyes and come back to reality. Congratulations! You have just completed your first lesson in the art of creative visualization. That's all there is to it. It's a simple form of escape you engage in for one reason and one reason only.

Creative visualization helps you to mold and shape a brand new life for yourself.

For instance, if you put yourself wholeheartedly into the above exercise, you may notice that you feel a little more relaxed or maybe even a little happier. That's because creative visualization is powerful. (If I had told you to close your eyes and imagine that you were eating a lemon, I guarantee you that your cheeks would have puckered as you anticipated the bitter taste.)

Creative visualization works because the images in your mind have an effect on your mental state. It really is that simple. If you want to feel better about what's going on in the outside world, you have to change the pictures you see inside your head.

But there's more to it than that. You can rely on a visual image to make yourself feel better at the snap of a finger. However, when it comes to the life you're leading, things are not going to turn around that quickly. In other words, if you feel sad, you can picture a happy experience and you will automatically feel happier. On the other hand, when you're trying to take control of your life, the changes you want to see occur aren't going to happen in an instant.

You must fill your mind with positive pictures of all the wonderful things you want. Do that for at least 15 minutes once a day or a few times a week and you will see a difference in a matter of months.

Basically, visualization helps you to attract what you want into your life. In many ways, visual images are like affirmations — in the form of pictures. It may seem hard to believe that a simple fantasy can change your world, but it can and does. The thoughts and pictures fluttering through our minds have the tremendous power to affect our future. You may not understand why but that doesn't matter. Most of us don't truly understand how pagers, cell phones and even TV sets work, but that doesn't stop us from using them.

We should remember that fact when we find ourselves questioning whether or not our mental pictures really can alter our destiny. Don't worry about it. Don't doubt it. Simply try it.

Most Olympic athletes enjoy sharing stories about how they "saw" themselves accomplishing an amazing feat before they actually won their gold medals. To become Olympic champions, they must practice everyday for hours. Yet many gymnasts and long distance runners place a great deal of value on the time they spend visualizing their bodies gracefully gliding over the balance bars or bounding swiftly across the finish line.

They are perfect examples of creative visualization at its best. Many of them owe their success to hard work, determination, belief in themselves and the ability to dream without losing faith.

If it works for them then surely it can work for you. The ability to dream is God-given. It's a gift bestowed on everyone at birth. What's more, it's free. You can dream as often as you like, as long as you like. There are no boundaries, no limitations and absolutely no strings attached.

God has given us all an open invitation to whatever we want out of life. It's up to you to place those desires in the center of your mind and build incredible fantasies. It's up to you to stay positive and focused enough to turn those fantasies into goals. It's up to you to hold on to a vision of yourself as the person you want to become.

As often as possible, play around with the images in your mind. Whenever you have a thought about anything, a picture always flashes in your brain. Examine those pictures. Are those the situations you want in your life? Are you imagining positive events or negative ones? Do you see yourself doing things that fill you with pride?

Pay attention to all the images that dance through your mind. If they aren't uplifting, get rid of them. Readjust that old, boring scenery. Add fun experiences and happy people and places that make you smile and tingle all over.

Think of the world as a lump of clay and yourself as a sculptor. The pictures flitting about your mind are a source of power. Use them to build any kind of life you want. Dream on!

———

VISUALIZATION EXERCISE

1. Gather as many old magazines as you can. For the next few days or weeks, flip through the magazines and look for pictures that reflect the type of life you would like to lead. If you dream about doing well in school and/or attending college, cut out pictures of students wearing caps and gowns. Look for pictures of young people in the career you would like to pursue and cut out pictures of them wearing professional attire or working on their jobs. Cut out pictures of any clothes you would like to own or the car you would like to drive. If you see a home you would like, cut that out too. When you're finished, paste or tape all of the pictures on a very large piece of cardboard or poster board. You are making a collage of the beautiful life you would like to create. Add positive affirmations or exciting words and phrases that you also cut out of magazines. Be sure to include a picture of yourself somewhere on the poster. Hang it on your bedroom wall and look at it often. It will motivate you and encourage you to dream and set goals.

2. Find a quiet place to sit, then close your eyes and picture something you want to see occur in your life. Do this for at least 15 minutes.

3. Jot down what you saw. Describe it in detail. How did it feel? Did it seem vivid and real? Practice this often and try to make the images very clear and convincing.

.

Chapter Six

God is Listening

"I'm not a nun or a priest but I don't really care what people think about me because only God can judge me and I think our relationship is pretty cool." (Queen Latifah, actress/rap artist)

———

Once upon a time, an elderly woman decided to pay a visit to a neighbor who lived several blocks away. As she arrived, she waved excitedly then took her time walking slowly up the stairs. The stairs creaked and the old woman began getting concerned. She moved even slower, being careful to hold on to the railing on the side of the porch.

Within a few minutes, her friend, Miranda, was greeting her. Laughing, Miranda hugged her and told her not to pay attention to the sounds. At that moment, the older woman glanced to her left. At the end of the long porch, was a large, brown dog, curled up in a tight ball. He moaned and that's when she realized that the stairs weren't creaking at all. The dog on the porch was responsible for the noise. He moaned again and again causing the woman to stare helplessly at Miranda.

"What's wrong?" she asked, bewildered.

"Oh, don't mind him," Miranda said. "He's just moaning because he's lying on a nail."

This remark really troubled the woman.

"But Miranda," she whimpered. "If your dog is lying on a nail, why doesn't he just get up?"

"Because he doesn't want to," explained Miranda. "It doesn't hurt enough yet."

Do the problems in your life hurt enough yet? Or are you still moaning, complaining and moping around the house? Behavior like that doesn't get us anywhere but we sometimes give in to it anyway. It is the easy thing to do. It doesn't require a lot of energy and, usually, if you do it long enough, you can get people to feel sorry for you.

Their sympathy will help you to feel okay for awhile but sooner or later, you'll feel out of it again. There is only one way to feel better. You have to stop moaning and get off the nail (or whatever nagging problem is sticking in your side). You have to decide enough is enough. You have to be so tired of hurting that finally you muster the energy to turn to God and talk to God like a personal friend.

You say something is really bugging you? Maybe it's something minor. It doesn't matter. PRAY! Get quiet inside and understand that God is always willing to hear whatever it is you have to say. Use the language you're comfortable speaking in. Whisper, sing, laugh, rap or simply chat with God like you're talking to a lifelong buddy.

That's who God is — the one who knows and understands and will meet you at whatever point you are in life. Quietly say:

"God, I just failed my math test."

"God, I'm feeling like nothing and I was just yelled at about nothing."

"I can't believe this God, but I just found out Cyndi was gossiping about me. Did you hear me, God? Cyndi! She was supposed to be my best friend. What's up with that?"

Or you can be simple and direct. Close your eyes or keep them open and softly say: "God, I really need you right now. Please send me a message." Remain quiet and wait, for you will receive an answer.

If you're feeling too upset to PRAY, you might want to go for a walk, do a few sit ups or jumping jacks or dance around your room awhile. The exercise will calm your mind. You will begin feeling relaxed and, when that happens, you are in a better state to receive God's guidance.

Now, understand that this guidance isn't going to be loud and it won't be accompanied by a lightning bolt or a burst of music. Hollywood has led us to believe that there is something mystical about connecting with a Higher Power. But if you're expecting to receive information from God in a cloud of smoke or clash of thunder, you'll be waiting a long time.

The voice of God is often known as your intuition or your inner voice. It is gentle, like a sweet, soft whisper. It is a surprise bit of knowledge that comes to you in a comforting message that is usually squeezed in between your own thoughts. It is so quiet that it is very easy to miss.

That is why so many of us don't hear it. God talks to us daily but we aren't listening because we are allowing worries and doubts to control our minds. The moment we release worry, we can pick up on God's ongoing advice. It might be the peaceful voice inside our head. It might be the kind words of a friend. It might be something we keep hearing over and over at church, at school or on the radio. Or it just might be something we hear in a song or on TV at just the moment when we were wondering what to do.

If you want to hear God loud and clear, the key is to get closer. Suppose your mom was calling you and you were downstairs talking on the phone to your girlfriend. You would hear her but you might not be able to understand what she was saying. You would have to hang up the phone and walk up the stairs. The higher you climbed, the clearer her words would become.

This is the same way it is with God. When we talk to God, the messages are a lot more clear when we are making an effort to get closer. We strengthen our relationship with God the same way we strengthen our relationships with our friends. We call them more often. We share our thoughts and secrets. We trust them.

If you consider God a friend, then treat God like a friend. Call God with the same frequency you call your boyfriend or your best girlfriend. It's real easy to get distracted by real people. It sometimes seems that no one is going to understand you more than the person who hangs out at the mall with you or sits next to you in your biology class.

The person who is sitting next to you may be the most dependable, trustworthy person you know. But that person is not God. Just because that person is part of the world you can see, feel and touch doesn't mean you should place more significance on him or her than you do on a Higher Power.

Understand that there is a beautiful world beyond this one. It is not a fantasy. It is real. It is magnificent. It is a place where you can turn to in silence when you meditate.

During quiet moments of meditation and prayer, you draw energy and power from this very peaceful place deep inside of yourself. God lives there. If you don't feel God's presence right away, be patient and make sure your mind is free of worry.

Try using an affirmation to quiet any troublesome ideas or thoughts of woe that might be racing through your head. (When you worry, you block your connection to God. God is talking and you can't hear a word. It's like God is at the top of the Empire State Building and you are down in the basement.)

Are you prepared to jog up the stairs and listen for God's direction? Then get off the nail and stop all the moaning! Life only hurts when you refuse to do anything about whatever is troubling you. PRAY. You have a friend named God who is always ready and willing and eager to listen.

———

PRAYERS

When we're feeling low sometimes it's hard to think of what to say to God. The following prayers are very simple, brief and easy to remember. Whether you're in the middle of your day or settling down for the night, a quick prayer of just a few words can bring great comfort.

Prayer for Faith and Self Esteem:
I believe in myself Dear God because I believe in you. I believe with all my heart in what you're preparing me to do.

Prayer for Support:
Dear God: I find strength in your presence. I am moving to do all I can and I realize you are doing all that I cannot.

Prayers for Trust:
I trust in you God and Dear God I know you are always with me, flowing through me, surrounding me, comforting my heart and spirit.

Dear God: In you I trust. Please make a way and remove these burdens from my heart.

Prayer for Guidance:
Dear God: The road ahead is sort of scary. I pray for your loving direction. Lead me, Guide me Dear God. Please show me the way.

Prayer to Ease Worry:
Peace flows like a river through my mind and my spirit and I thank you Dear God that I am one with you.

Prayer for Comfort and Security:
Help me not to complain, Dear God. Help me to understand. Help me to reflect your light, Dear God. And, Dear God, please hold my hand.

Prayers for a Broken Heart:
Dear God: The ache I feel is so hard to bear. Help me to realize that it will not last always. Show me a brighter future.

Dear God: I need your comfort and your understanding right now. Help me to believe that the pain I feel will not last forever. Help me to deal with it, Dear God. I surrender my disappointment to you. Please comfort me and and fill my heart with hope.

Prayer to Ease Pain:
Dear God: The more I resist, the worse I feel. Help me to let go and allow you to handle this sorrow. Help me to understand that you are taking care of me and that I have nothing to fear.

Dear God: I need your help to cope with this sadness I feel. Help me to see that better days are ahead. Assist me, Dear God, for I don't know what to do.

Dear God: I am journeying down a road I've never walked before. It is unfamiliar and it doesn't feel very good at all. Please ease these awful feelings. Help me to realize that this pain is temporary but your love is always.

Prayer to Deal With Loneliness:
Dear God: You're holding my hand. Help me to hold yours. Continue to nudge me and reach for me. Remind me that as long as you are with me, I am never alone.

Dear God : Sometimes I forget you are here watching me and supporting me. Nudge me when my mind wanders into worry and fears of loneliness. Remind me that you are always with me and that I am never alone.

Dear God: Fill me with your presence, Lord. Flood my heart and soul with your light. Shine through me and help me to feel your constant comfort and your ongoing love.

Prayer to Love Others:
Dear God: Your love never ends but my patience and my love sometimes run out. Please grant me the compassion and understanding to love even when it's hard.

Chapter Seven

FORGIVENESS: A BAND-AID FOR THE HEART

(Healing/Forgiveness Affirmation)
"I release all disappointment from my mental, physical, spiritual, and emotional body, cause I know that the spirit guides me and love lives inside me. That way, I take life as it comes."
(INDIA.ARIE, singer)

———

Picture this: It's a hot summer day and you have just received a big present from a cousin. You open the box and uncover a bundle of cozy-looking, winter clothes.

They are beautiful items, custom-made especially for you. So you decide maybe you should wear them now. Despite the fact that it is ninety degrees outside, you proceed to put on a thick, long-sleeved sweatshirt, a pair of corduroy jeans, bulky socks and heavy, lace-up boots. Then, you slip into a baggy, cardigan sweater and a denim jacket. Next, you button on a heavy, winter coat with fur lining and a huge hood. Before stepping outside into the heat, you add a final touch — two wool scarves and a pair of insulated gloves.

Well, I can't say how this is affecting you but I'm getting very warm just thinking about it. And if you're a normal, active, human teenager (who just happens to be from this planet and not from Mars) I'm sure you'd be pretty miserable dressed like that during the summer.

All of those extra clothes would be a major burden. They would weigh you down and you'd probably feel really heavy.

You'd overheat. You'd sweat. You'd walk around all that day in an extremely bad mood.

That is until someone looked at you like you were crazy and asked why you were wearing all that stuff in the first place. At that point, you might snap out of it and begin peeling off layer after layer of clothing. Your answer (if you weren't too dizzy to talk) might be something like: "Well, this stuff was given to me so I felt as if I absolutely had to wear it all."

Does that sound ridiculous? Of course it does. Yet, it is a fair representation of what many of us do everyday. Something happens to us and weeks later we still feel obligated to wear the anger. We wear it on our faces. We wear it in our emotions. We store up bitter feelings and then we wear them in our spirit.

Some of us haven't discovered that just because someone gave us a painful experience doesn't mean we have to cling to it. We can take it off, like an old costume. We can shed it like a lizard sheds its skin. How? All we have to do is FORGIVE.

There is an enormous power and peace that comes over us when we learn to FORGIVE. For the first time in our lives, we feel free. It's like wearing shorts and a tank top when the sun is shining — instead of a box load of winter outfits. It's like waking up in the morning fresh and happy and so full of positive energy you can't wait to get out of bed.

Of course, you won't experience these wonderful feelings unless you try it. So why not try it? FORGIVE someone. Don't get caught up in the notion that you're letting someone off the hook. Actually, just the opposite happens. You let yourself off the hook.

Think about yourself wearing all those unnecessary clothes on a humid day. That's exactly what it is like when you carry around the burdens and pains of someone else's past actions. If someone does something to you, don't add it on, just like you did when you added the sweatshirt, the sweater and the coat. If you do, it will build and build and before you know it, you're bogged down. You're unfocused. You're cranky. And you're uncomfortable. All because you refuse to stop wearing the stuffy garments of someone else's actions.

Recognize that FORGIVENESS is not a gift you give to the other person. IT IS A GIFT TO YOURSELF! You have made a choice to FORGIVE so you are the one who gets to feel the joy. You are the one who gets to feel relaxed, happy and peaceful. That's because you have literally removed layers of pain, anger and resentment. You have stripped off attire you didn't need in the first place.

Look at it this way. When someone does something to you, it hurts. If you refuse to forgive, you are saying: "Yes, you hurt me and now I am going to hurt myself further by holding on to that memory. By getting angry every time I think about it, I am agreeing to give you the ultimate power of hurting me for the rest of my life."

If you choose this attitude, you are not hurting your enemy. Instead you are stewing and brewing and allowing those feelings to creep around inside of you. You aren't allowing yourself to feel good. It's as if the person who wounded you just handed you a contract requesting permission to inflict more pain — and you are signing on the dotted line.

You might as well send them a letter that reads: "Dear enemy: You dogged me and I'm going to be mad forever. So you go on and be as happy as you can. I'm never going to be truly happy because I'm going to let the memory of what you did haunt me at times. I'll probably have a nasty temper and a chip on my shoulder. Or I might just let it prick me now and then like a thorn.

But hey, you have fun. You have taken away my power so I have no choice but to bundle myself up in gloomy thoughts like an overdressed person sitting around in lots of clothes on a real hot summer day!"

Sound silly? Don't laugh. That basically sums up the attitude of anyone who allows a bad experience to mess up their attitude, their day, their week and even their lives.

Years ago, I had the opportunity to live in Harare, Zimbabwe, which is next to South Africa. While there, I visited many game reserves and national parks. During one visit, a group of students and I noticed that a large number of monkeys had gathered together in the trees where they could peer and jeer at us. Monkeys are mischievous creatures. Out of the blue, some of them began throwing things at us. They threw sticks, twigs, rocks, anything they could get their hands on.

Fortunately, they were a very bad aim and no one was hurt. It simply became another experience. None of the members of my group made much of it. We simply laughed and moved on. We weren't angry. We didn't say: "Look at those horrible creatures. We'll never forgive them for almost ruining our trip."

They were wild critters looking for something to do. We didn't hold their actions against them. They were cute, innocent, little monkeys. They didn't know any better.

Now, let's take this a step further. How do any of us know for a fact that anyone knows any better? You don't have to be a monkey to make a mistake or to confuse right with wrong. Do you know anything about the pasts of the people who may have injured you in some way? Do you know about their backgrounds or even the way they think? You don't.

That's why it's best to let it go and allow God to determine another's fate. You are not judge or jury. You are simply a teen-age girl searching for a way to make sure your own life is as productive and positive as possible.

You are searching for the road to joy and beauty and it's hard to find it when your mind is cluttered with bothersome thoughts about what someone did to you yesterday or one day way back when. You can't heal yourself as long as you're wasting time worrying about someone else.

Suppose you went to the doctor and told him that your best friend deliberately pushed you down a flight of stairs and broke your big toe. The doctor would wrap bandages around your toe. Then the doctor would prescribe pain medication.

But what if the entire time the doctor was telling you how to take care of your toe, you continually complained about this friend and how awful she was?

The doctor might say: "Don't worry, I'm going to tell you how to heal this toe and make it just like new." In which case, you could reply: "But doctor, you don't understand. This girl is terrible. I still can't believe she did this!"

The doctor could ignore you or he could become exasperated and say: "I'll tell you what. Let's forget about your toe. Bring me the girl who pushed you and I will bandage her toe instead."

That's not going to help you very much is it? Your toe isn't going to heal if the doctor puts a bandage on the person who pushed you.

The same thing applies to other situations. You can't heal your own spirit if you spend too much time fretting about another's actions.

FORGIVENESS is the best Band-Aid. Try it. For if you do, you will find that healing will take place. No, it won't be the other person who is mended.

The wounds you patch up will be in your own heart.

FORGIVENESS EXERCISE

Have You Forgiven Someone Lately?

Write down the names of all the individuals who have wronged you in some way. Then, write a brief note telling them that you forgive them. Tell them that you understand that only people who are in pain can hurt others. Look at the list several times a week for at least a month and practice feeling sympathy for each person. Set yourself free by saying, "I forgive you."

Chapter Eight

THE ATTITUDE OF GRATITUDE

"God has got to smile on you a whole lot of times for you to get where you're going. . . That's why I never start a show without saying how good God is to me." (Steve Harvey, comedian)

———

Lucky You! You are so fortunate to have… Wait, let's back up a minute. What, exactly, do you have to be excited about? Think about it for a while. I'm sure you can come up with a few things here and there. (You might even have a list as tall as a CD tower.)

Are you in good health? Then, you have been blessed with the joys of a comfortable existence. You can walk, run, see and hear. Physically, you are pain free.

On the other hand, you just might be experiencing a stay in the hospital or grappling with the effects of a long-term ailment. If that's the case, you may notice that there are other blessings flowing through your life. Your parents may be exceptionally loving and dedicated. Or you may possess the gift of a kind heart, a sparkling personality, a brilliant mind, a musical talent.

No matter who you are, life hasn't forgotten you. Everyone has at least one thing they can feel good about. And everyone has many reasons to call upon this wonderful source of power known as GRATITUDE.

GRATITUDE is a healing, positive state of mind. It is like a prayer. When you feel grateful, you are letting God know how appreciative you are for all He has given you. You are giving thanks and acknowledging God's goodness. You are also putting yourself in a position to receive more.

It works like this: The more grateful you are, the happier you are and the happier you are, the more positive your thoughts. Do you remember the comments made about positive thoughts in earlier chapters? They are a signal to God that you are tuned in and turned on to His power. You are a believer. And you are ready to attract more blessings.

Imagine a wild and crazy, roller coaster ride. It is so exhilarating with all the hills, the ups, the downs, the dips, the speed! It seems that one good feeling leads to another, then another and another. That's the way it is when you are feeling thankful about whatever good things, however small, have landed in your life. When you focus on the good, it multiplies. (When you focus on the bad it multiplies too, so steer your mind toward happiness and gratitude.)

When you do, you will find yourself receiving more and more and more.

Think of a small child, a seven-year-old girl for example. What if you gave her a new doll for Christmas and she told you she didn't like it? Suppose she pouted and cried and threw the gift on the floor. I don't know about you but I'm not sure I would put a whole lot of effort into another present any time soon.

On the other hand, I have presented toys to children who smiled and thanked me and showered me with hugs. Something about their joy makes me want to keep sharing with them. Their happiness triggers a happy feeling inside of me. I feel good that I made them feel good. Their show of appreciation encourages me to give to them again and again.

And so it is with us. We turn people off when we wear sad faces and walk around saying everything is "wack." When we zero in on what we don't like, we make ourselves miserable.

But, when we are cheerful about what we already have, life tends to reward us with even more. So what's it going to be? Are you going to complain and waste energy focusing on what is missing in your life?

Or are you going to be positive? All you have to do is constantly remind yourself that every negative situation has another side. And that side often is happy and upbeat. Remember, the rain is followed by a rainbow.

Say to yourself "There may be some things lacking in my world but there's some good stuff here too." Then keep looking for it. It may be something you overlooked — like a best friend, a favorite aunt or uncle or a surprise, new earrings or a personal greeting card you received in the mail.

Get in the habit of searching for a special blessing everyday. Be on the lookout for it and I promise that if you dig deep enough, you will find it. Practice thanking God on a daily basis for all the gifts you have received. If you only find one, that's okay. Simply become aware of the presence of God and say a silent prayer of thanks for that one, small present. (You might even want to jot it down and keep a daily list.)

This may seem like no big deal at first, just something different to do. But as they say in the Nike ad, "Just do it!" And keep doing it. I promise that within a couple of months, something is going to start happening.

That tiny list of three blessings is going to eventually grow into about seven or eight blessings. A few months later, you might count 15 additional blessings in your life. A year from now, who knows?

GRATITUDE EXERCISE

1.Save precious tokens and souvenirs that represent fond memories. For instance, a concert program or concert ticket stubs or a photo of yourself wearing your favorite outfit or simply looking your best. You can also find a photo of yourself doing something fun like traveling, cheerleading or participating in a team sport. Hold on to trinkets given as gifts or even a flower someone gave you. (Press it between wax paper or plastic wrap to preserve it.) Put these items in a box (a shoe box or some other box). On top, write the words: Treasure Chest. Whenever you need a little cheering up, pull out the items and look at them.

2. How many blessings do you have to be thankful for? Think of as many as you can and list them.

3. Also, try keeping a gratitude journal. Everyday, keep track of all the things that made you happy and all the special blessings you received. This exercise, practiced daily, will make you feel good about your life. As time goes on, your daily list will get longer and longer. Watch and see!

Chapter Nine

GIRL IN THE MIRROR

"My journal has helped me stay in touch with who I essentially am." (Jewel, singer/actress)

———

I grew up in a modest eastside Detroit neighborhood where games and laughter were commonplace. Everyday, all the kids on the block would gather together for one heart pounding adventure after another. Usually, we romped and ran free but, occasionally, we would form teams to participate in organized outdoor activities like "Red Light/ Green Light," "Hide and Go Seek" and "Tag."

I still remember how much fun those games were — especially during the long hot summer months when we were out of school. We raced up and down the block for hours, switching from one game to another.

I enjoyed most of them. But there is one I disliked so much that it stands out in my mind to this day. However, when I think about the game now I often smile because it serves as a reminder of how important each individual is to her team, to her family and to society.

The game was known as Red Rover. Each team would form a long line and lock hands. Then, they would face the other team. That team was also standing in a line with their hands locked into a tight grip.

The next step was very crucial. Someone on one team would glance at the opposing team, select a teammate (let's say Sally), then shout: "Red Rover, Red Rover, send Sally over." At that point, Sally would abandon her team then run as fast and hard as she could in an effort to break through the human barrier formed by the opponents.

Sally would focus on one set of hands and arms and use all of her might to try to break through. If she was successful, she could then choose someone from that team to take back to her team. If she wasn't successful, she was forced to stay and join the other team.

In the end, the team with the strongest arms would grow and grow and eventually win the game because there was no one left on the other side.

Now, what does this have to do with you? Plenty. The tightly gripped hands and arms in the game of Red Rover symbolize a chain. Each link has to be strong or the chain itself is not strong.

For instance, think of a gold chain or another type of chain that people often drape around their necks. It doesn't matter how beautiful or how expensive the chain is. If one link is weak, the chain will break. So what that most of the links are durable, strong and mighty. All it takes is one fragile section and the chain will not hold together.

And so it is with life. We are all links in a magnificent human chain and we are all connected in spirit. If one of us is weak, if one of us is petty, if one of us is angry, bitter or lazy or spiteful, then the entire chain is affected. The chain of humanity will suffer because it contains too many inadequate links.

That's why we use the term "girl in the mirror." When you look at yourself and take responsibility for your own actions, you are doing all you can to became a powerful, mighty link in the chain that joins us all.

In fact, you should consider jotting your feelings in a journal each night. A journal is an effective way of keeping track of personal attitudes, reactions and emotions. It's also a way of getting to know yourself better. The better you know yourself, the easier it is to pinpoint your strengths and weaknesses. The more you pinpoint your strengths and weaknesses, the easier it is to transform yourself into the positive and radiant young woman you have always wanted to become.

So keep your focus on the only person you can change — yourself. Have you ever heard Michael Jackson's song "Man in the Mirror?" There is significance in the lyric: "If you want to make the world a better place, take a look at yourself and make that change."

The change has to start somewhere. When you make a vow to improve yourself, you are helping to shape the entire planet — one individual at a time. Remember that the next time you struggle with a decision to do your homework or to cut class, to tell the truth or to criticize a friend.

Your actions are helping to make the chain of life stronger and more brilliant. Or you are engaging in behavior that will inevitably turn you into a weak link.

The choice is all yours.

———

Mirror Exercise

1. List personality traits that you would like to improve. For example, if you have a habit of complaining, write that down. Or if you have a tendency to be envious of others, write that down. When you finish, write down instances when you made the best of things instead of complaining or times when you were able to resist feelings of envy.

What happened to make a difference? For instance, what did you say to yourself to chase away the envious attitude? What did you do to help yourself remain positive instead of negative? Do this exercise for each quality you would like to change.

2. Keep a diary. (It could be a spiral notebook or a journal.) Write down your feelings or day to day experiences and note how much you are changing and improving.

Chapter Ten

THE GAME OF A LIFETIME

"Each year, I've learned that much more about myself. I guarantee I'll be a totally different person next year from who I am now."
(Tiger Woods, golf pro)

———

Here's a game worth checking out. Pick one day and spend it keeping track of your positive and negative thoughts. It doesn't matter which day of the week it is. All that matters is your willingness to discipline your mind.

It actually is a lot easier than it sounds. In fact, it can be a lot of fun. As soon as you wake up in the morning, grab a notebook and draw three lines to create three columns on one sheet of paper. At the top of one column, write the words: NOT SO GOOD; on the next, write: BETTER, and on the third, write: THE BOMB!

For the rest of the day (in between your classes and whenever you get a break at school) you're going to keep track of your thoughts. No, you can't fit all of your thoughts on one page. But you can make note of your dominant thoughts and place them in the appropriate category.

Simply record any thoughts of sadness, criticism, jealousy or resentment under NOT SO GOOD. Under BETTER, jot down the thoughts that feel okay or that you simply feel indifferent about. They are just random thoughts, neither good nor bad. Now, I don't think I really have to explain which thoughts should appear under THE BOMB!

Those are the happy thoughts, the confident thoughts, all the peaceful, loving thoughts that make you feel good inside. Keep track of them and watch them grow in your mind.

After an hour, you will begin feeling enthusiastic and powerful.

You might not like everything you're thinking about. But you'll certainly get a charge out of standing guard over those thoughts. So do it with gusto. If you find it tough squeezing this exercise into your school day, simply try it one weekend or try it once in the morning and again when you return home from school. Examine your thoughts and boldly decide which ones you should let live and which ones need to be kicked out.

Your mind is like a garden and this game is showing you how to pull out the weeds. Get the picture? Good, because there's more. Find another notepad or flip to the back of this book to the pages designated notepaper. Prepare to keep this book (or notebook) with you all day. After lunch, say 12:30 or 1 p.m., begin drawing slanted lines every time you notice an unhealthy or self-defeating thought. Anytime you think "I can't do that" draw a line. If you catch yourself saying "I'll never be any good at this" or anything else about yourself that is less that flattering, draw another line. After you have noticed four negative thoughts, you should have four slanted lines. On the fifth negative thought, the fifth line should be a slash through the other four.

For instance:

////

Then start over. By bedtime, you're probably going to have quite a few groups of four lines with slashes through them. Don't worry if your notebook looks something like this:

//// //// //// //// //// ////

And don't get too cocky if it looks like this:

//// ////

We all have good days and bad days. You are on the road to turning the bad days to good days by learning to manufacture good thoughts. You are on the road to learning just how exciting it is to become a member of the thought police.

Before going to bed, check out what you wrote in the morning.

Did your thoughts change as the day went on? Keep your results then play the game again and compare the outcome. (If you don't want to keep tabs on paper you can simply pay attention to how long you can go without having a complaint or thinking anything negative, critical or sad. This is what I call the top dog approach. Just try to make sure you don't let any negative ideas survive in your mind for longer than five minutes. They are going to try to creep in but your goal is to catch them right away.)

Policing your thoughts might sound a bit tough at first. But keep doing it. Gradually you will get better and better. It will be like watching a baby learning to walk. The baby plods along eagerly as if nothing can discourage him. He takes one step, falls and gets right back up. He tries and tries again.

That's the way it is trying to manage your thoughts. It's easy to use expressions like: "I am the master of my destiny." But when things start falling apart in our lives, we might forget that we are in control. We forget to pray. We forget to do our affirmations and we forget that we can improve our lives by making sure we are thinking in a way that is upbeat and positive.

You will stumble at times so be patient. No matter how hard you try, your new attitude probably won't be achieved overnight. It takes practice and it takes patience.

Just like a baby, you have to take one small step at a time. Go at your own pace and be gentle with yourself. Don't get upset and don't give up if you get angry or depressed. So what that you spend a day thinking useless thoughts? For every one day like that, you will probably have a thousand inspiring, happy days.

You have to remind yourself that everyone gets ticked off sometimes. The key is not to focus on the times you failed or the times when you were down. It's best to remember all the times you succeeded.

As a matter of fact, that's exactly what the baby does. If a baby focused on all the times he tried to walk and fell down the poor little thing would never try again. But the baby remembers that special moment when he almost took seven steps. That memory is what keeps him giggling and trying.

No matter how many times he falls, the baby plasters that big grin on his face and gives it another shot. As we get a little older, we tend to forget to approach life that way. For some reason, we start concentrating on our mistakes and not on our victories.

But if you switch that around and focus on the victories instead of the mistakes, you will feel 100 percent better.

All you have to do is think of something that will immediately put you back on track. A friend of mine once told me that whenever he sees a pair of suspenders, he is instantly reminded that God is always holding him up. Another friend wears a camel pin on his jacket. He said the camel begins his day on his knees and ends his day on his knees. Therefore, the camel pin serves as a constant reminder to him to pray.

Symbols like that are triggers which give us the jolt we need and help us regain our focus. Come up with a trigger — a prayer card you carry around, an affirmation, a piece of jewelry or a picture that reminds you of a goal. Use these triggers every time you need a boost.

Also, when you feel like you have been far too negative, quickly whisper a positive thought to yourself. (One positive thought can cancel out dozens of negative ones.)

Never give up! You are a beautiful diamond and right now you are learning how to glitter. For true gleam and spark, you are going to have to rely on your new, high-quality thoughts. Be proud of them. Cherish them. And don't forget to polish them daily.

Now, go out into the world and shine!

~ ~ ~